A GARDEN STYLE BOOK

Terrific Tomatoes

· · · · · · · · · · · · · ·

[SIMPLE SECRETS FOR GLORIOUS GARDENS—INDOORS AND OUT]

MIMI LUEBBERMANN
PHOTOGRAPHY BY FAITH ECHTERMEYER

CHRONICLE BOOKS

SAN FRANCISCO

Library of Congress Cataloging in Publication Data
Luebbermann, Mimi
Terrific tomatoes: simple secrets for glorious
gardens, indoors and out / by Mimi Luebbermann;
photography by Faith Echtermeyer.
      p.   cm.
"A Garden Style Book."
Includes bibliographical references and index.
ISBN 0-8118-0551-4
1. Tomatoes. 2. Cookery (Tomatoes). I. Title.
SB349.L8 1994
635'.642–dc20   93-6088
                                     CIP

Printed in Hong Kong

Cover and interior design by
Aufuldish & Warinner

Distributed in Canada by Raincoast Books,
112 East Third Ave., Vancouver, B.C. V5T 1C8

10 9 8 7 6 5 4 3 2 1

Chronicle Books
275 Fifth Street
San Francisco, CA 94103

Contents

TOMATOES TO GROW IN CONTAINERS 37

TOMATOES TO GROW IN THE GARDEN 47

GROWING EXOTIC VARIETIES OF TOMATOES 61

FRESH TOMATOES IN THE KITCHEN 75

INTRODUCTION

Far away in the warm, damp, tropical forests of Peru, plants with little currant-sized fruits grow in wild abandon. These humble ancestors bear little relation to the shapely platter-large or midsize, pear-shaped or cherry globes we know as tomatoes. The native Americans who over some two thousand years chose seeds from the more desirable, larger fruits started a long transformation.

¶ Today's stylish aristocrats descend from a further four hundred years of European and North American tinkering with plant breeding. Now tomatoes grow successfully from Alaska to Florida, in the short growing season of Maine, the long, muggy summers of South Carolina, and the searing heat of Texas. Their colors range from solid luscious red to pinks, yellows, and greens, or striped in oranges, reds, and two-tone green. Their tastes range from sugar sweet to tart and lemony. Anyone who has taken a round, blushing, ripe homegrown tomato in hand mar-

vels at the beauty, scent, and ultimately the flavor of a tomato picked at its peak and eaten within hours before its sugar has turned to starch.

¶ The tomato is a member of the Solanaceae family, and its far-ranging cousins include petunias, eggplant, potatoes, and the deadly nightshade, which flavored the homicidal brews of history and made everyone just a bit nervous. Mentioned first in literary history in the mid 1500s, the tomato was sporadically written about mostly in terms of its supposedly poisonous qualities or its horticultural merit as a pretty plant. However, if the historians were not harvesting and cooking it, a host of gardeners were breeding, improving, and savoring the fruit. Even so, given the look of the homely, lumpy fruit that migrated back to America in the 1600s, the dubiousness of its reputation is not difficult to credit. Although the earlier yellow varieties had been bred to the red that's known commonly now, these ocean travelers were corrugated and bumpy, not the perfect spheres we know today. The tomato gained grudging acceptance with a considerable effort in public relations, including advocates' public consumption of tomatoes by the hatful to prove their edible nature. Slowly, slowly, tomatoes began to win approval in the kitchen, and breeding continued to improve their look, taste, and habits. Now

Lycopersicon esculentum is not only common but the gardener's favorite "vegetable."

¶ Tomatoes have long since become, to use the current lingo, grower friendly. They produce in copious quantities when their variety matches the climate and soil of a backyard; pairing the natural instincts of the tomato to your garden is the first step toward a successful harvest. Numerous strains have evolved to permit close pairings anywhere. Some of the newer varieties of tomatoes grow in small spaces. The determinate varieties are being bred as smaller and smaller plants to tuck into corners or grow in containers. Everyone can enjoy the flavor of their own-grown tomato.

¶ If growing tomatoes is a pleasure, eating them is a delight. All the new colors and shapes invite you to try different culinary combinations, and whether you stuff them with goat cheese, Southern-style stew them, grill them for smoky salsas, or just slice them to eat with a drizzle of olive oil, your homegrown tomatoes will sing with a flavor unmatched by any supermarket variety. Some recipes worthy of classic status in your repertoire are included at the end of this book.

¶ I must have met my first tomato somewhere in my childhood on the family farm in Virginia. The fragrance of the crushed tomato leaf is

deeply rooted in my memory from wandering down the rows of tomato plants, which I recall towering above me. After kettles steamed in the cool, dark basement kitchen, there were neatly aligned rows of quart jars bright red with stewed tomatoes. Tentatively, I began to grow the plants in the long, cool growing season of Oakland, California. Like a miracle the plants grew, flowered, and fruited. Eating one still warmed with sun made me a missionary.

¶ An adventurous neighbor began growing seeds from a catalogue, and he introduced me to the world of tomatoes outside the nurseries. As though having rounded a corner, I had suddenly at hand myriad different, ever more delicious varieties. Chatting with someone at a nursery, I learned about planting early, midseason, and late varieties to stretch out my harvest.

¶ Along with elaborating these basics for you, I have summarized tomato-growing techniques learned from the experiments of all the years since my own shaky beginning. Using the gardening know-how embedded here is like tomatoes themselves, which start by returning a harvest of a few good fruits, then suddenly multiply their production for you by the bushel basket. When you know how, the pleasures of growing tomatoes can draw you into a lifelong pursuit of culinary gusto.

CHARACTERISTICS OF TERRIFIC TOMATOES

Though tomatoes have been considerably altered through centuries of seed selection and twentieth-century hybridizing, some of their basic nature remains. Tomatoes are tropical plants; warm climes are their truest homes. Scientists have managed to make tomato plants easier to grow, but they have not changed their basic needs. Like beach-goers, tomatoes want sun and warmth whenever they can get it. Wise gardeners will imitate the tropical climate as much as they can.

¶ Tomatoes will not grow if night temperatures drop below 50 degrees, making both air and soil temperature too cool. Various techniques can be used to heat the tomato plant, fooling it into believing in kindly, warm Peruvian days and nights. The use of cloches, glass covers, or plastic will warm up the small tomato plants like miniature greenhouses until summer's heat does it naturally.

¶ Although in the right climate tomatoes survive as perennials, they are grown as annuals. The seed is sown in early spring, and the plants bloom, fruit, and die or are pulled up by the end of the season.

¶ The indeterminate tomatoes are the ones that need to be pulled up, since they grow and fruit for as long as they have the requisite warmth without interruption by frost. They have green, ripening, and ripe fruit on the same plant. In mild climates, they will continue to grow until a killing frost. When the term "vine" is applied to tomatoes, it refers to the tendency of indeterminate varieties to put out long branches; they need training and staking to maximize harvest.

¶ The alternative type is the determinate varieties, which grow one crop of fruit over a short harvest period. All the fruit on the plant ripens at about the same time. When determinate varieties are preferable, it is for their smaller size; they take less space. The term "bush" is a descriptive label for the short stems of the plants, from eighteen inches up to only four and a half feet. Determinate varieties are especially good for containers because of their small size. To extend a determinate crop, plant varieties that mature at successive harvest dates, as described below.

¶ Semideterminates too are beginning to appear in catalogues and nurseries. They have the growth habit of the determinates, staying relatively short, but like the indeterminates, they produce fruit over a longer season. These dwarf indeterminates boast a full season of continuous production like their taller cousins and are becoming invaluable to gardeners who grow tomatoes in containers or small spaces.

¶ Tomatoes have been bred for specific environmental requirements, so there are hundreds of different tomatoes available for you to grow. Narrow your choices by first identifying a wide range of varieties that boast great flavor. Then, to pick the variety to grow, consider three main factors: habit of growth and also, as described in the next section, disease resistance and time of harvest. Tomatoes are hybrid varieties or they are open-pollinated, also called old-fashioned or heirloom. Hybrid varieties may be more disease and pest resistant, with high yields, but are sometimes less tasty. Seed companies today have realized the home gardener's preference for tomatoes that sing with taste and have a finely honed balance between sugar and acid. Old-fashioned varieties were saved for years by home gardeners because of their superior flavor, and now they are again commercially available to you. Hybridizers are working to breed resistance but save the taste. If you have a garden free of soil diseases, you may be able to grow some of these types.

¶ The flavor of tomatoes is enhanced by sunshine, the leaves turning nutrients into sugars that are stored in the fruits. When your tomatoes are left on the vine to ripen and the warm summer sun shines on the leaves, completing the complex chemical process, the taste is fully developed. Cooler climates produce less-sweet tomatoes.

¶ When you choose your tomatoes, be aware that the yellow and pink varieties seem milder in taste than the red, and some people find them bland in comparison. The naturally green varieties have a pleasing combination of acid and sugar, and they are increasing in popularity as people come to know them.

¶ Seeds and plants are available in the early spring from nurseries, garden centers, and specialty garden shops. Often, the variety of seeds and plants is limited. If you have the time and patience, you may want to try growing your own plants, ordering seeds from mail-order catalogues to secure some of the more interesting and unusual varieties now available. Harvesting a tomato from a plant that you started with a one-sixteenth-inch seed makes a connection to the other tillers of the soil, in a direct line with all those planters who have been growing tomatoes for going on twenty-four hundred years.

About growing terrific tomatoes

ven for those new to raising home-grown bounty, tomatoes grow easily, their deep green foliage shooting up to fill wire support cages or climb to the tops of trellises. Remember that you will have the best success with varieties that are resistant to diseases and suited to your climate.

Water in Soil

¶ Plants grow with a circulation system that uses water to carry nutrients from the soil up through the stem to the leaves, flowers, and fruits. Water flows up through the plant to the leaves, and as the water is evaporated from the leaves, more water is drawn up from the roots, like a straw sucking up liquid.

¶ During periods of high evaporation, such as hot or windy days, the rate of water lost from the leaf increases, so the plant pulls more water in through the roots and up through the stem. When the plant loses more water than it can quickly replenish, it wilts. A properly watered plant is one that has constant access to readily available water in the soil. Make sure to increase your watering during hot and windy days.

¶ Soil composition affects the amount of water that soil retains for plants. Very

sandy soil drains quickly, so plants have less water available; clay soils drain less readily. The air in the spaces between the soil particles contains the same gases as our atmosphere, and the roots breathe in oxygen. When soil is filled with water, oxygen is pushed out and consequently is not available to the roots. Just as plants can die from too little water, they can also die from too much overwatering or poor drainage, or both. Normally when an area of soil fills with water, gravity pulls the water down through the soil pores, allowing oxygen to fill them in again. Certain factors, such as the lack of a hole in a planting container, the use of rocks at the bottom of a planting container, or very heavy soils, prevent this process and cause poor drainage and suffocation. Even though it is traditional to add rocks or crockery to the bottom of containers, the new convention is to ignore that century-old instruction and just fill the container with potting soil. Adding the layer of larger-size particles actually sets up a barrier, making container watering less successful.

¶ Adding plenty of organic matter before you plant is a way to improve soil composition and drainage, and avoid problems caused by poor soil. You can use your own homemade compost, or purchase aged compost to dig into the soil. In sandy soils the organic matter retains moisture; compost absorbs water like a sponge, then holds it available for the plants. In clay soils the compost breaks up the clay particles, improving particle size and creating spaces through which water can drain.

WATERING TOMATO PLANTS

¶ Tomatoes are easy to grow, but they require regular watering to develop healthy, tasty fruits. To send water directly to the roots, bury near the stem of the tomato, when you plant it, a one-foot piece of plastic pipe or a juice can with one end cut out and the other pierced with holes. Leave one or two inches of the watering pipe or can above the soil so you can find it easily when the plant is larger. Commercially available "tomato

boosters" work the same way to channel the water where the plant needs it the most. Water early in the day at the soil level to avoid encouraging bacterial or fungal diseases, which thrive in the damp. Do not overhead-water tomatoes, because fungal spores can be splashed from the soil to the leaves of the plant.

¶ Container plants need particular attention when watering. Containers exposed on all sides to wind, shimmering heat, and sun can dry out very quickly, and sometimes it is difficult for the gardener to tell that the potting mix under the plant is rock hard and dry until the plant goes into stress, with leaves turning a gray tone and all the branches wilting. A drip irrigation system can be invaluable in maintaining a regular supply of water to the plants. Monitor container plants very closely to make sure water is sinking in throughout the container, not just running out the sides because the potting mix has dried out completely. When this problem occurs, let a hose drip very slowly for at least one hour into the container, or until you can dig down below the soil level and find the mix moist.

¶ In the spring and early summer, when tomatoes are growing rapidly, plan to water generously. To avoid growth prob-

lems, water regularly and thoroughly and do not allow your tomatoes to dry out and wilt before you water again. Erratic watering can cause blossom-end rot, splitting, and other problems that interfere with fruit growth. When the plant is beginning to set fruit, gradually lessen the amount of water you give it so the fruit flavor becomes more concentrated.

SOILS, POTTING MIXES, AND PREPARED GROUND

¶ Soil is a mixture of the three soil particles–sand, silt, and clay–plus any organic matter. Sand is chemically inactive, so it is the clay and silt and the organic matter that are involved in the complex exchanges of water and plant nutrients. Sand, however, is by far the largest in size of the particles, so the presence of sand means that there will be correspondingly large spaces between soil particles. These very large soil pores contribute to fast drainage, high oxygen concentrations, and good vertical water movement.

¶ The organic matter in soils is mostly old plant material, decomposing under constant attack by bacteria and fungi. Over time, these liberate mineral elements that are essential to plants for their growth. The bacteria and fungi feeding

on the organic matter are thus beneficial to the health of the plants, and these microorganisms further add to their health by fighting off other microorganisms that cause plant diseases.

¶ Use of a good-quality potting mix for growing tomatoes in containers is critical, for a soil medium that retains moisture, drains well, and does not become concrete hard later in summer. Commercial potting mixes have been sterilized, and for gardeners with disease-infected soils, these mixes allow tomatoes in containers to grow without risk of infection.

¶ For planting in the ground, prepare the soil two to three weeks before your transplants are ready to set out. If the soil is so wet that it falls off the shovel in clumps, you will have to wait to get started or risk compacting the ground, making it rock hard.

¶ First remove existing plant material, such as weeds or plants that you no longer want to grow there. With a shovel, a spade, or a machine such as a rototiller, add four inches of compost or other amendments, and turn the soil over to a depth of twelve to eighteen inches. Water the turned soil and allow any undesirable seeds that may be in the ground to sprout. At a time when the ground is damp but

not soggy, remove the unwanted plant material once again. Using a hoe or shovel, break up any clods and rake the surface smooth for planting.

GROWING SEASONS

¶ Tomatoes grow, flower, and fruit at different rates according to their specific variety. Early-season tomatoes set fruit quickly despite cool temperatures, producing those anxiously awaited first tomatoes before summer temperatures rise. Because of the cooler weather, not as much sugar is developed in the plant, and so these early tomatoes may not have full flavor or the sweetness of tomatoes grown in the height of summer. Mid- and late-season tomatoes need warmer temperatures to develop flowers and set fruit.

¶ When you buy your seeds or plants, notice their growing season or the number of days from transplanting until they fruit. Catalogues always give this information, and plant tags in nurseries usually have it somewhere on the front or back. Many seed packets do not give you this information. If it is not on the packet, and you do not recognize the specific tomato variety, you are better off not buying the seeds.

¶ Gardeners living in cool climate areas must select early-season tomatoes to get any fruit. If you have a short growing season, cherry tomatoes and the early-season varieties will still reward you. Try some of the special growing techniques to get a rush on the season (p. 48). If you live in areas with long hot summers, plant early-, mid-, and late-season varieties to ensure a long succession of harvest (as described on p. 50).

¶ Very-early-season tomatoes produce ripe tomatoes in from 50 to 65 days, midseason varieties in from 65 to 80 days, and late-season in from 80 to 110 days or more.

STARTING FROM SEEDS

¶ Starting your own tomato plants from seeds is easy, and it offers you the advantage of growing a wide range of varieties that nurseries do not stock. If you live in a cold climate with a short growing season, starting seeds inside produces vigorous plants that are ready for transplanting when the ground warms up. Tomato seeds can be sown directly into the ground later, after the summer's warmth has brought the ground temperature up to a level that encourages germination. Order your seeds in January to make sure

you start with fresh, high-quality stock. (Some seed sources are listed p. 90.)

¶ Check at your nursery for choices of seed starting kits, such as plastic six-packs or peat pots. Styrofoam flats or six-packs have individual separations for each plant and transplants pop out of them easily. Some gardeners use heat mats placed underneath germinating trays to keep the soil evenly warm.

¶ Seeds need an environment of between 65 degrees and 75 degrees to germinate. Sprouts will pop up in six to eight days. A sunny south window may provide enough warmth and light, or you can use Gro-lights or full-spectrum lights adjusted to four to six inches above the containers. If your plants lean toward the light source and look skinny and weak, they are not getting enough light.

¶ Start your tomato seeds six to eight weeks before you want to put plants outside into the ground or containers. You can buy potting mix or you can make your own formula from equal quantities of vermiculite, perlite, and peat moss. It is important to use sterilized potting mix to avoid diseases that infect seedlings. To make sure the plants get off to a good start, add nutrients to the potting mix. You can follow the directions for a good-quality pelleted tomato food, or water with a low-nitrogen fertilizer diluted to half-strength once every week after the seedlings are one inch high.

¶ Thoroughly moisten potting mix with water before planting. Add the mix up to one inch from the rim. Space the seeds about half an inch apart and cover with a quarter inch of the mix. Pat this down firmly. Keep the mix just moist but not soggy to avoid encouraging fungal infections. The first two leaves on the plant are called cotyledons, and they are oval shaped. They are followed by the development of the first set of true leaves that will grow into characteristic-looking tomato plant leaves. When the little plants have grown at least three sets of true leaves, they are ready to transplant—only into a bigger container if the weather is still cold or if night temperatures fall below 50 degrees. You can wait longer to transplant, but make sure to do it before the roots begin to creep out the bottom of the container. After transplanting them, begin a program of fertilizing every two weeks with a low-nitrogen liquid fertilizer.

TRANSPLANTING

¶ Because young tomato plants grown indoors or in a greenhouse are very tender, you need to accustom them to the more variable outdoor temperatures before you plant them outside. Keep the young plants outdoors during the day only, for one week before you plant them. Start them in the shade and then gradually move them into the sun. When you plant them, do it in the late afternoon, to lessen the stress caused by the heat of the day.

¶ Tomatoes develop roots along any part of the stem that is in soil. Roots will grow out from the buried stem, increasing the size of the root ball and thus the health and productivity of the plant. When you are ready to transplant your tomatoes, remove the cotyledon leaves and bury the plant up to the point where the next set of leaves grows. Very tall leggy plants should be planted the same way, even if it means putting much of the plant underground. You can also root any part of the established plant throughout the season; just cut a three-inch side stem or sucker above the first set of leaves, and plant it.

¶ In the cooler days and nights of spring, young plants will grow more quickly with added warmth. Four plastic milk containers filled with water set surrounding each plant will create a solar heater to speed growth until warmer days arrive. Special warming devices, such as Wall O' Water or plastic wrapped around the bottom of a wire support cage, will also increase day and night temperatures.

THE DEEP HOTBED HOLE METHOD

¶ For years, gardeners have argued about different ways to ensure an early tomato harvest, and the waiting for the first ripered tomato of the season is a time-honored tradition of impatience. In the late 1800s, market gardeners fashioned hotbeds as a way of planting early in spring when nights were still nippy and days cool. As soon as the ground could be worked, they dug their hotbeds, layering fresh manure, fresh green material such as prunings and weeds, and well-aged compost. The action of the decomposing layers warmed the ground so that early spring crops grew regardless of the weather. Home gardeners have adapted this technique to raising backyard tomatoes in order to get a jump on the growing season and early harvest for the kitchen. In climates with a very short growing season, this technique is invaluable for producing fruit before the first freeze.

¶ To be successful, you must start a hotbed hole just as soon in the spring as you can work the soil, but remember, if your soil is so wet that clumps fall off the shovel, you must wait until it dries out. Working soil when it is too wet compacts it, forcing out the oxygen and space between the soil particles that allow plant roots to breathe.

¶ To try the method, dig a hole three feet deep by two feet wide. Fill the hole up to one foot of the rim with layers of fresh or aged manure, straw, garden clippings, compost, and either one-half cup each bone meal and wood ashes or a good-quality pelleted tomato food. Water the layers well. Cover the layers with twelve inches of soil, and mark the site of the hole. Continue with this process, spacing the holes two feet apart and the rows three feet apart. Wait at least for two weeks before planting and measure your results in your harvest.

PLANNING BEDS AND PLANTERS

¶ In planning your tomato garden, consider your space requirements and your planting techniques. If you want to grow in containers, you can have compact form with determinate plants, which take less space but do fruit over a short period of time. To extend the harvest period, plant varieties that fruit in differing numbers of days. Indeterminate plants need more training and staking in containers but will continue to fruit over a longer period.

¶ If you plant indeterminate varieties in wire cages, you can plant them two to three feet apart. If you are using determinate varieties, you can plant them in cages spaced eighteen inches apart. Some gardeners mix their determinate varieties into their perennial flower borders because they have a tidy growth habit and look decorative hung with brightly colored fruits.

¶ Study the tomato types. Plant the little cherry-sized or baby-pear-sized varieties and collect buckets every week. Grow tennis-ball-sized fruits with either determinate or indeterminate varieties when you have a short summer growing season or limited space. The large sauce tomatoes and the beefsteak types demand hot climates to grow to their one-pound or more size and develop the intensely sweet flavor so wantonly tomato. Be sure to include early-, mid-, and late-season varieties of these. Try the different shapes

and colors that are available, and experiment with different growing techniques.

¶ If you have the space, five or six plants will keep your household in tomatoes all summer long. One cherry type and one small pear type will give you a salad and snacking supply. Add two cooking/paste types, one midseason and one late season, if your climate allows. Two slicing varieties also chosen for color and for succession will round out your tomatoes harvest, providing you with supply and diversity.

FERTILIZERS

¶ The major nutrients needed for plant growth are nitrogen, phosphorus, and potassium. A plant removes these nutrients from the soil and uses them to grow. Fertilizer added to the soil replaces the missing or used-up nutrients, allowing the plant to continue its growth. Nutrient needs are greatest during periods of rapid growth, typically spring and summer. Tomatoes need less nitrogen than most other plants, and a soil rich in nitrogen will cause tomatoes to grow luxuriant foliage and fewer fruits. Tomatoes need greater quantities of potassium and phosphorous in their soil for fruit production.

¶ Generally commercial fertilizers list their contents as the percentage of each nutrient in the order nitrogen-phosphorus-potassium, so a standard 20-10-10 fertilizer would be 20 percent nitrogen (too much for tomatoes), 10 percent each phosphorus and potassium. The ingredients are always listed in this order.

¶ Phosphorus and potassium are necessary for a wide range of tomato plant functions, especially during periods of rapid growth. When you plant your young tomatoes be sure to add a source of phosphorus and potassium to the planting hole, so the nutrients will be right where the roots can absorb them. Adding a half-cup of wood ashes from your fireplace and a half-cup of bone meal (in containers, half as much) will provide organic nutrients necessary for tomato production, or use a synthetic fertilizer either in liquid form, to be diluted according to the directions on the label, or pelleted. If your soil is very alkaline, you need to use half the amount of wood ashes called for in the directions. If you choose to use synthetic fertilizers, either liquid or solid, make sure you use one with a combination such as 5-10-5 to fulfill the special nutrient needs of tomatoes. Keep up a routine of fertil-

izing container-grown plants with a diluted, low-nitrogen liquid fertilizer every two weeks. If you want to garden organically, look for organic liquid fertilizers that are low in nitrogen.

FROST PROTECTION

¶ Fleshy plants like tomatoes with soft stems are particularly susceptible to frosts, especially when just transplanted into the soil. Set a plastic jug with the bottom cut off over the top of each young plant for frost protection; take it off during the day if the weather warms to above 70 degrees, since under the jug your plants would burn. The commercial product Wall O' Water has protected plants down to 10 degrees in tests.

¶ If you have a row of plants to protect, flex plastic fiberglass panels into tunnels or cover arches with plastic to maintain warmer night temperatures. Keep tunnel ends or sides open to allow air circulation during the day. Prevent plant foliage from touching plastic to avoid burning the leaves.

PESTS

¶ For the home gardener, there are a few pests that will damage or destroy tomato plants. To diagnose a problem, look carefully to determine whether your plant damage is from insects or bacterial or fungal diseases. There are a number of pests that make inconsequential holes in leaves but whose destruction does not weaken the plant or affect the fruits. If you have a serious infestation, consider one of the new insecticides that do not leave long-term residues on your plants or in your soil. I recommend that you use these pesticides only, and only when your crop is severely threatened. If you are unsure of the problem, check with your county agricultural extension agent or your local nursery before you attempt to eradicate it.

¶ The easiest damage to diagnose is from tomato hornworms. With these you will notice holes in the leaves and fruit, and sometimes tiny black pebbles, or frass, on the leaves. Look for a long green caterpillar with a hooked horn at the end of the body. Another caterpillar, the tomato fruitworm, will eat into your tomatoes but generally does not affect the leaves. Handpick the caterpillars and destroy.

¶ Small aphids may be seen sucking on the stems of the tomato plants or on the backs of the leaves. Either squash them with your hands or wash them off early in

the morning with a jet of water. Tap the leaves to eject droplets left behind and promote quick drying.

DISEASES

¶ Microscopic organisms cause fungal and bacterial diseases in tomatoes. Once the soil is infected with these diseases, it is difficult to grow many tomato varieties. Tomato breeders have come to gardeners' rescue by hybridizing plants with resistance to these very destructive plant diseases. When you order seeds or buy plants, look for varieties that are labeled "VFN resistant." If your soil is severely affected, plant other crops that are less susceptible and grow tomatoes in containers with sterilized soil.

¶ "V" and "F" stand for resistance to wilt diseases, which besides causing plants to wilt, eventually cause their death. Keeping your plants correctly watered and fertilized will help their resistance. When you are sure of your diagnosis, remove the plants immediately and dispose of them in the garbage. Do not attempt to compost the vines or you will spread the disease.

¶ Verticillium wilt is a soil-borne fungus that has no cure. Your plants will suddenly begin to wilt at the tips of the plants and will not recover even after watering or evening cool.

¶ Fusarium wilt is a soil-borne fungus that shows as a yellowing of the plant leaves. It starts at the base and moves upward. Like verticillium, it has no cure.

¶ The "N" signifies resistance to nematodes, microscopic worms that live in some soils. They attack roots, preventing plants from growing naturally. Plants that stop growing and have nodules on the roots are infected with nematodes. To help combat these harmful worms, add plenty of organic matter to the soil. The decomposing compost introduces beneficial bacteria and fungi to the soil, and these microorganisms feed on the destructive nematodes.

¶ Experts suggest that if you have root diseases you should avoid growing tomatoes or any member of the Solanaceae family for three years or more, in the spot where the disease occurred.

BLOSSOM DROP

¶ Plants will drop their blossoms if night temperatures are too low or too high. Early-season varieties are bred to withstand temperatures of less than 50 degrees, but most midseason and late-season varieties will suffer blossom drop if the night temperature falls below 50 degrees or rises above 75 degrees. If the temperature is too low, protect the plants with night caps or portable greenhouses, or cover their cages with clear plastic. If you live in areas of high heat, choose the special tomato varieties developed to set blossoms at higher temperatures.

MULCH

¶ Mulch is one of the gardener's best tools in growing tomatoes successfully. By adding a layer of insulation to the soil, it keeps soil temperature constant, seals in moisture, and inhibits weeds; it also adds organic matter to the soil. Straw, compost, grass clippings, or wood chips are good materials for mulch. Add a three- to four-inch mulch around the stem of the young tomato once the ground has warmed up in summer. If you add mulch too soon, it will act as an insulator, keeping the ground from warming and slowing the growth of your tomato plants.

¶ Some gardeners prefer to use sheets of black plastic as a mulch around the base of their tomato plants or along a row of plants. This type of mulch has the merit of raising soil temperatures slightly as well as providing weed cover and mois-

ture control. Plastic mulches do not add any value to the soil, either in nutrients or organic material.

TRAINING, PRUNING, AND SUPPORT

¶ The training of tomatoes presents special challenges. Without a doubt, tomato training is also a hotly debated subject, with new studies exposing some old-fashioned techniques as faulty, confirming others, and proposing still other new techniques to increase yield. You must know whether you are growing determinate or indeterminate tomatoes to select the best training techniques, because the pruning and support with which you train them differ for the two types.

¶ Determinate tomatoes grow only to a certain height, so pruning them to control size is rarely necessary. Provide low support to keep their fruit off the ground and prevent slug and snail damage or loss of fruit from ground contact.

¶ Indeterminate tomatoes continue to grow throughout the season, so you need to train them in order to contain their growth and support the trailing stems.

¶ Tomato plants grow with a central stem and horizontal branches that extend from it, and the fruit is borne on sprays off

both the stem and branches. From the crotch where the branch joins the stem, another kind of branch, called a sucker, shoots out. New research reports that the yield of the plant is not affected by the suckers being pinched off, but that if they are the plant will set fruit sooner. If you want very-early-season fruit, pinch out the growing tip of the sucker above the first set of leaves. You can prune off the whole sucker to control growth, but since if you do not it too will provide fruit, some gardeners choose to leave suckers on.

¶ Especially the indeterminate varieties of tomatoes need the support of stakes, trellises, teepees, or wire cages as they grow. Tall and leggy, the branches can be broken by the weight of their fruit; many of these as well as the main stems need staking. Even the determinate varieties, although shorter, may need support as the fruit grows. The clusters of ripening tomatoes can be too heavy to be carried without breaking branches or resting on the ground. Strips of soft cloth or plastic horticulture ribbon are best to tie the plants loosely to stakes, trellises, and teepees.

¶ One of the most successful training methods is to use the cylindrical cage that's made from concrete-reinforcing wire. Most hardware stores carry this wire, and you will find that its six-inch-square holes make it the most convenient through which to pull out a tomato. The wire is also very strong, so it will not collapse under the weight of the tomato and its fruit. Simply roll the wire into a circle and fasten it securely with wire twists.

¶ Some nurseries and catalogues are offering cages that flatten for storage after use—a real convenience. I do not recommend the small wire cones because they are insufficient to handle all but the smallest determinate varieties. Look for the largest cages available.

THE LAST HARVEST

¶ Inevitably, summer draws to a long golden close, fall beckons with cooler days and chilly nights, and your tomatoes begin to ripen more slowly. As night temperatures threaten frost, pull up your vines and hang them inside a warm place by their roots. Although not all their fruits will ripen, many will continue to develop to ripeness in the warmer temperatures, not with the sweetness of full summer but still tastily, and in keeping with the inevitable *tristesse* of summer's end.

TOMATOES

TO GROW IN

CONTAINERS

If you have at least six hours of sunlight a day, you can produce tomatoes from containers. Tomatoes are naturally very deep rooted, so look for containers that are as deep as possible.

Either determinate or indeterminate varieties will be smaller grown in containers and will produce fewer tomatoes. Most still need some form of staking or wire cages. If you have sunny wall space available, you can set up a trellis and grow the tomato up your wall. ❧ Keeping tomatoes correctly watered is the most difficult aspect of container planting, since the plants' roots have less soil volume to draw upon, for water and for nutrients. Water on a consistent schedule. Check with your fingertip that the soil is damp only, not still soggy, before watering. Water more often when temperatures exceed 80 degrees. Elevate your container on a saucer filled with gravel or marbles so that the bottom never rests in water, which would encourage root rot. ❧ If you have a drip system to irrigate your plants, you are assured of a consistent watering pattern that never lets the potting mix totally dry out. Alternately, cut out the top of a metal juice can, either a pint or a quart size (the bigger the container, the larger the can you need), and with a hammer and a nail, make several small holes in the bottom. When you transplant, bury this alongside the tomato plant to within an inch of the rim. Water by filling up the can several times. ❧ The better-formulated potting mixes have a texture and composition that help water soak in and drain thoroughly, and your plants will grow better in them. Mulch the top two inches of the container with sphagnum moss or straw as an additional means of retaining moisture in the soil.

TOMATOES IN A HANGING-BASKET GARDEN

*U*rbanites who depend on their neighborhood grocery stores for tomatoes wrapped in cellophane have a wonderful experience in store. A sunny outside porch, rooftop, or window ledge can support a hanging garden that supplies salad-ready cherry tomatoes all summer long. Both determinate and indeterminate varieties produce quantities of candy-sweet tiny tomatoes in a hanging basket and without staking. Do rotate the plant to ensure even growth. ¶ **HOW TO DO IT** ¶ In the spring, after the last chance of frost, you can safely plant your tomatoes. When plants have three sets of true leaves, they are ready to set out. Make sure to harden them off for a week, by leaving them outside in a protected area during the day and bringing them inside at night. Before planting, submerge the transplants in their containers in a sink or bucket of water until air bubbles cease to appear. ¶ Choose a hanging container 12 inches in diameter and at least 12 inches deep, with drainage holes in the bottom. Fill this container to within 2 inches of the top with potting mix, and soak the potting mix with water until it is thoroughly moist. For each plant, scoop out a hole in the center of the container. To the bottom of the hole, add ¼ cup each bone meal and wood ashes, or follow the directions for a good-quality pelleted tomato food. Set the plant into the hole and pack the potting mix around the plant up to the first set of true leaves. Pat down the surface and water to fill in any air pockets. Hang the container in a location where it will receive six hours of sun a day. ¶ Make sure to keep the soil moist but not soggy, and fertilize with a low-nitrogen liquid fertilizer solution every two weeks.

Lycopersicon esculentum

❧

What You Need
Cherry tomato plants, bought or grown •
Hanging container 12 inches in diameter and
at least 12 inches deep for each transplant •
Potting mix •
¼ cup each bone meal and wood ashes per
plant, or a good-quality tomato food •
Low-nitrogen liquid fertilizer

❧

Recommended Varieties
Basket King Hybrid, Burpee's Pixie Hybrid,
Early Cherry, Red Cherry, Small Fry

❧

Growing Conditions
¼ to a full day of direct sun

❧

When to Buy
Seeds: in winter and spring from catalogues
Plants: in spring from nurseries

❧

When to Plant
Seeds: inside, 6 to 8 weeks before spring's
last frost; Plants: after the last frost, when
nights do not fall below 50 degrees

❧

When to Harvest
60 to 70 days after transplanting

❧

Pink, Gold, and Red in One Container

Part of the joy of growing tomatoes today is the wide range of colors, patterns, and flavors available. Fruits in a bouquet of colors are as decorative as flowers in full bloom. ¶ Growing a melange of tomatoes in the same container is most successful when you plant only determinate varieties with the same modest growing habits, unless the containers are larger than 5 gallons. Choose plants that will fruit in about the same number of days in order to produce a multicolored table-ready harvest. ¶ For this arrangement, make sure to add a wire cage or staking. ¶ **HOW TO DO IT** ¶ In the spring, after the last chance of frost, you can safely plant your tomatoes. When plants have three sets of true leaves they are ready to set out. Make sure to harden them off for a week, by leaving them outside in a protected area during the day and bringing them inside at night. Before planting, submerge the transplants in their old containers in a sink or bucket of water until air bubbles cease to appear. ¶ Add the potting mix to a fresh container with drainage holes in the bottom. Water until it is thoroughly moist. For each plant, scoop out a hole that is 8 inches wide and 8 inches deep or at least twice as wide and twice as deep as the current container. Add ¼ cup each bone meal and wood ashes to the bottom of the hole or follow the directions for a good-quality pelleted tomato food. ¶ Gently remove the plant and its potting mix from its container. Set the plant and the mix into the prepared hole. Pack extra potting mix around the plant up to the first set of true leaves. Pat down the surface and water to fill in any air pockets. Set up a wire cage, stakes, or other support. ¶ Keep the container in a location where it will receive at least six hours of sun a day. Make sure to keep the soil moist but not soggy, and fertilize with a low-nitrogen liquid fertilizer every two weeks.

Lycopersicon esculentum

❧

What You Need
2 or 3 tomato plants, bought or grown • Potting mix • Container at least 20 inches in diameter and 18 inches deep for 2 plants, or at least 24 inches in diameter and 24 inches deep for 3 • ¼ cup each bone meal and wood ashes per plant, or a good-quality pelleted tomato food • Stakes or a wire cage • Low-nitrogen liquid fertilizer

❧

Recommended Varieties
In smaller containers: Basket King Hybrid, Burpee's Pixie Hybrid, Chello Hybrid, Floragold Basket, Gold Nugget, Green Grape, Husky Cherry Red •
In larger containers:
Pink Pearl, Red Pear, Yellow Pear

❧

Growing Conditions
¼ to a full day of direct sun

❧

When to Buy
Seeds: in winter and spring from catalogues
Plants: in early spring from nurseries

❧

When to Plant
Seeds: inside, 6 to 8 weeks before spring's last frost; Plants: after the last frost, when nights do not fall below 50 degrees

❧

When to Harvest
About 70 days after transplanting

❧

A COMPOST CIRCLE OF TOMATOES

Recycling leaves and garden prunings has become a way of life even for city gardeners, no matter how small the backyard. Sitting through the winter, the compost circle decomposes enough to become a soil medium for a tomato planting. In late summer, when your garden begins to die down and the tomatoes finish, break up your tomato circle, toss it to mix the layers, and spread it over the garden beds as mulch and compost for the following year. ¶ **HOW TO DO IT** ¶ During the fall, start your compost container for the following year. Form a circle with a diameter of about 3 feet. Use wire that is 4 feet wide so your compost wire circle will be 4 feet tall. Add leaves, green weeds, and garden clippings in layers, building your pile as high as you can since it will sink down as the material decomposes over the fall and winter. Add layers of garden soil and wood ashes if they are available. You will need a compost pile that is still at least 3 feet tall by the time you are ready to plant. ¶ After the last chance of frost in spring, you can safely plant your tomatoes. When plants have three sets of true leaves, they are ready to set out. Make sure to harden them off for a week, by leaving them outside in a protected area during the day and bringing them inside at night. Before planting, submerge the transplants in their containers in a sink or bucket of water until air bubbles cease to appear. ¶ For each plant, dig a hole in the compost near the edge that is 8 inches wide and 8 inches deep or at least twice as wide and twice as deep as the container. Add ½ cup bone meal and ½ cup wood ashes, or follow the directions for a good-quality pelleted tomato food. ¶Gently remove the plant and its potting mix from its container, and set it into the prepared hole. Fill the hole with extra potting mix and pat down the surface. Water to fill in any air pockets. Keep ✐

Lycopersicon esculentum

What You Need
2 tomato plants, bought or grown •
Concrete reinforcing wire 4 feet wide and 6 feet long, tied in a circle 3 feet in diameter •
Leaves, green weeds, garden clippings •
½ cup each bone meal and wood ashes per plant, or a good-quality pelleted tomato food • Potting mix • Low-nitrogen liquid fertilizer •
Stakes, if plant height requires

Recommended Varieties
Cherry size: Basket King Hybrid, Burpee's Pixie Hybrid, Early Cherry, Red Cherry, Small Fry, Supersweet 100
Midsize: Early Girl, Dona

Growing Conditions
¼ to a full day of direct sun

When to Buy
Seeds: in winter and spring from catalogues
Plants: in spring from nurseries

When to Plant
Seeds: inside, 6 to 8 weeks before spring's last frost
Plants: after the last frost, when nights do not fall below 50 degrees

When to Harvest
70 to 80 days after transplanting

the soil moist, but not soggy—the compost will drain more quickly than soil—and fertilize with a low-nitrogen liquid fertilizer every two weeks. If the plants grow taller than the wire, add stakes to support them.

A TOMATO HERB GARDEN

It is difficult even to think of cooking or eating tomatoes without teaming them in savory herb combinations. A grouping such as two basil plants, one Italian parsley, and one thyme will provide you with enough of this complementary set for general household use. Plant the herbs close to the edge of the container so they will spill over the sides as they mature. As your tomato plants grow, pinch off the bottom leaves and branches for ten to twelve inches above the ground to make sure the plants do not shade the herbs.

¶ **HOW TO DO IT** ¶ In the spring, after the last chance of frost, you can safely plant your tomatoes and herbs. When tomato plants have three sets of true leaves, they are ready to set out. Make sure to harden them off for a week by leaving them outside in a protected area during the day and bringing them inside at night. Before planting, submerge the transplants in their containers in a sink or bucket of water until air bubbles cease to appear. ¶ Choose a 24-inch container with drainage holes in the bottom, and fill it to within 2 inches of the top with potting mix. Soak the potting mix with water until it is thoroughly moist. Scoop out two holes in the container deep enough to plant the tomatoes up to the first set of true leaves and 1 foot apart. Add ¼ cup each bone meal and wood ashes to the bottom of each hole, or follow the directions for a good-quality pelleted tomato food. Set the plants into the holes and pack the potting mix around the roots up to the first set of true leaves. Pat the surface down firmly, and water. ¶ Scoop out holes around the outer edge of the container twice as deep and twice as wide as the herbs' pots. ✈

Lycopersicon esculentum (tomato)•
Ocimum basilicum (basil)•
Petroselinum neopolitanum (Italian parsley)•**Thymus vulgaris** (thyme)

❧

What You Need
2 tomato plants, bought or grown • 4 herb plants, such as basil, Italian parsley, and thyme•Potting mix•Container at least 24 inches in diameter and 24 inches deep•¼ cup each bone meal and wood ashes per plant, or a good-quality pelleted tomato food•Stakes, if harvest is heavy•Low-nitrogen liquid fertilizer

❧

Recommended Varieties
Determinate tomatoes: Celebrity, Husky Gold, Husky Pink, Orange Pixie, Superb Super Bush
Herbs: Any, suiting your kitchen

❧

Growing Conditions
¼ to a full day of direct sun

❧

When to Buy
Seeds: in winter and spring from catalogues
Plants: in early spring from nurseries

❧

When to Plant
Seeds: inside, 6 to 8 weeks before spring's last frost; Plants: after the last frost, when nights do not fall below 50 degrees

❧

When to Harvest
75 to 95 days after transplanting

❧

Gently remove each herb plant from its pot, keeping its potting mix intact, and set the top of the root ball just at soil level. Fill the hole with extra potting mix and pat down the surface. Water to fill in any air pockets. The determinate tomato plants will probably not need support, but plan on adding a stake and loosely tying up the branches if your harvest is heavy. ¶ Place the container in a location where it will receive at least six hours of sun a day. Make sure to keep the potting mix moist but not soggy, and fertilize with a low-nitrogen liquid fertilizer solution every two weeks.

TOMATOES

TO GROW IN

THE GARDEN

The first cool breath of evening may be just stirring when you walk out to the garden to pick a bowlful of fresh tomatoes for dinner. The scent of herbs drifts in the air, yellow scallop squash

glow in the fading light, and tall corn rustles in the long rows. Everywhere you look, there is a lushness and a sense of summer's fertility. ✤ Growing tomatoes in the garden is easy if you remember the basics of cultivation. Choose a variety that suits your climate, amend the soil with plenty of compost, feed the plants with potassium and potash (from either organic ingredients or a commercial tomato food), and water consistently. When you think that within ten weeks a tiny seedling may grow to be six feet high with juicy, ripe tomatoes hanging from it, you can understand how crucial it is for the plant to receive steady nourishment. So before you set in your plants, be sure to dig eighteen to twenty-four inches down into the soil, mixing in lots of compost or other soil amendments to improve the texture. ✤ Plan your tomato garden to be as colorful as a bed of bright zinnias. Grow your plants in fanciful fashion; espalier them over garden walls, team them with contrasting colors, grow sunburst yellows with oranges and pinks to make a rainbow wall. Consider all the different shapes, and try some of the Cinderella varieties with their bumpy surfaces and heavenly flavor. ✤ If you have lots of space, you can plan a long season of harvest with indeterminate varieties. If you have less room or do not wish to provide cages or stakes, try the determinate varieties. Look at ways to grow the greatest variety and quantity in the smallest amount of space. Plan your harvest to last the whole summer, and try out new varieties every year.

A REALLY EARLY TOMATO PATCH

Carl Duncan

To be the first on the block with ripe tomatoes takes a bit of preparation. Browse your seed catalogues over the December holidays. Choose extra-early-season varieties with the shortest maturation dates, and send off for those seeds before your holiday decorations are back in the attic. While you wait for your seeds, set up an indoor incubation nursery. When you serve fresh tomatoes on Memorial Day, you will be a hero indeed. ¶ **HOW TO DO IT** ¶ Start seeds as soon as you get them (as described on p. 25). As soon as the weather allows, create a deep hotbed hole (p. 26) to start the ground warming. In preparation for planting, use a Wall O' Water or wire cages wrapped in clear plastic above the hotbed hole to warm the soil from the top down, or if you are planting in rows, stretch clear plastic over hoops. ¶ When your seedlings have three sets of true leaves, transplant them into 4-inch containers, burying them up to the bottom of the first set of leaves. When they have added another four sets of leaves, transplant into 6-inch containers. Check the bottom of the containers after two weeks, and when you see roots through the bottom holes, transplant each young plant into a 1-gallon container. Feed with a liquid fertilizer diluted half-strength, once a week. ¶ After the last chance of frost, dig a hole within the hotbed that is 12 inches wide and 8 inches deep. Add 1 tablespoon more of bone meal and 1 tablespoon more of wood ashes to the bottom, or follow the directions for a good-quality pelleted tomato food. ¶ Submerge the transplants in their containers in a sink or bucket of water until air bubbles cease to appear. Gently remove ✒

Lycopersicon esculentum

What You Need
Seeds of extra-early-season tomato varieties • 1 hotbed hole per plant • ½ cup plus 1 tablespoon each bone meal and wood ashes per hotbed hole, or a good-quality pelleted tomato food • Protective solar heating devices such as Wall O' Water or plastic sheeting • Stakes or wire cages

Recommended Varieties
Extra-early-season varieties: Early Cascade, Early Girl, Oregon Spring, Stupice, Sub Arctic

Growing Conditions
¾ to a full day of direct sun

When to Buy
Seeds: in winter from mail-order catalogues

When to Plant
Seeds: inside, 10 to 12 weeks before spring's last frost • Plants: 2 weeks to 1 month after you create the hotbed hole, with covers

When to Harvest
60 to 70 days after transplanting, as early as Memorial Day in mild winter climates

the plant and its potting mix from its container, and set it into the prepared hole so that the first set of true leaves is at the soil level. Fill the hole with soil, packing it gently around the roots. Pat down the surface, and water. ¶ Cover the tomato with its solar heating device. Continue to keep it protected until the weather warms to 60 degrees in the daytime and does not drop below 50 degrees at night. Set up wire cages, stakes, or other support when weather warms if you have not done so before. Make sure to keep the soil moist but not soggy, and fertilize with a low-nitrogen liquid fertilizer every two weeks.

A SUMMER-LONG TOMATO GARDEN

Plant a harvest that will last all summer long. Savvy gardeners choose the tomatoes they are going to grow first by the length and heat of the growing season and then by taste; the varieties recommended here are listed for all three factors. Pick out early-, mid-, and if climate allows, late-season varieties in your garden to extend your picking pleasure from June—if you live in a mild winter climate—or July until the first fall frost. ¶ **HOW TO DO IT** ¶ In the spring, after the last chance of frost, you can safely plant your tomatoes. When plants have three sets of true leaves, they are ready to set out. Make sure to harden them off for a week, by leaving them outside in a protected area during the day and bringing them inside at night. Before planting, submerge the transplants in their containers in a sink or bucket of water until air bubbles cease to appear. ¶ In prepared soil that is thoroughly moist, dig a hole for each plant that is 8 inches wide and 8 inches deep or at least twice as wide and twice as deep as its container. Add ½ cup each of bone meal and wood ashes to the bottom of the hole, or follow the directions for a good-quality pelleted tomato food. ¶ Gently remove the plant and its potting mix from its container, and set them into the prepared hole so that the first set of true leaves is at the soil level. Fill the hole with soil, packing it gently around the roots. Pat down the surface and water to fill in any air pockets. ¶ Add stakes or support the plants with wire cages. Keep the soil moist but not soggy, and fertilize with a low-nitrogen fertilizer every two weeks. Once the weather has warmed the ground, mulch each plant with 3 to 4 inches of organic compost in a circle 12 inches across.

Lycopersicon esculentum

What You Need
Tomato plants, bought or grown • About 6 square feet of prepared ground per plant • ½ cup each bone meal and wood ashes per plant, or a good-quality pelleted tomato food • Stakes or wire cages • Low-nitrogen liquid fertilizer • Organic compost

Recommended Varieties
Cool or short summer: Oregon Spring, Santiam, Stupice, Sweet 100 •
Cool summer evenings with warm days until October: Bragger, Carmello, Celebrity, Dona, Early Girl, Early Pik, Sweet 100 •
Warm summer: Celebrity, Early Girl, Large, Solar Set, Sweet 100 •
Long hot summer: Celebrity, Early Girl, Large, Solar Set, Sweet 100

Growing Conditions
¼ to a full day of direct sun

When to Buy
Seeds: in winter and spring from catalogues
Plants: in early spring from nurseries

When to Plant
Seeds: inside, 6 to 8 weeks before spring's last frost • Plants: after the last frost, when nights do not fall below 50 degrees

When to Harvest
52 to over 110 days after transplanting

Training tomatoes on a trellis or wall

Indeterminate varieties of tomatoes produce gangly vines that surge up to the sky, a result of old habits from jungle days. Some of the Sweet 100 plants grow over ten feet tall, Better Boy lunges out of the top of six-foot wire cages, and Park's Whopper seems to grow one inch a night. ¶ If you live in cool summer areas, training tomatoes to a trellis or wall, or similarly a fence or arbor, improves your harvest because you expose the fruits to more sun. With their brightly colored fruits, the plants make a focal point in the backyard garden while using space efficiently in smaller urban spaces. ¶ Successful trellising requires a weekly routine; prune suckers from the crotches where branches join stems and prune any branches that shield other branches you want exposed to sun. In hot summer areas, do not prune back the side branches too vigorously or your tomatoes may develop sunscald. ¶ Fasten branches to their supports with strips of soft rag, horticultural ribbon, string, wire, or raffia. Make loose loops to hold up the vine, because as the plant grows the stems will become larger and will need extra room to expand. If you tie the stems tightly you can cut off the circulation of the plant. When your plant reaches the top of the structure, snip off the growing tip to control growth. ¶ **HOW TO DO IT** ¶ In the spring, after the last chance of frost, you can safely plant your tomatoes. Plants with three sets of true leaves are ready to set out. Make sure to harden them off for a week, by leaving them outside in a protected area during the day and bringing them inside at night. Before planting, submerge the transplants in their containers in a sink or bucket of water until air bubbles cease to appear. ¶ In prepared garden soil that is thoroughly moist, dig a hole for each plant that is 8 inches wide and 8 inches deep, or at least twice as wide and twice as deep as its container. Add ½ cup each bone meal and wood ashes to the bottom of the hole, or follow the directions for a good-quality pelleted tomato food. ¶ Gently ✒

Lycopersicon esculentum

❧

What You Need
1 tomato plant, bought or grown, for each
2 horizontal feet of prepared ground ·
½ cup bone meal and wood ashes per plant,
or a good-quality pelleted tomato food ·
Trellis, fence, wall, or arbor ·
Low-nitrogen liquid fertilizer ·
Organic compost

❧

Recommended Varieties
Indeterminates: Better Boy,
Climbing Trip-L Crop, Giant Tree,
Oregon Star, Park's Whopper,
Red Cherry, Sweet 100

❧

Growing Conditions
¼ to a full day of direct sun

❧

When to Buy
Seeds: in winter and spring from catalogues
Plants: in early spring from nurseries

❧

When to Plant
Seeds: inside, 6 to 8 weeks before spring's
last frost · Plants: after the last frost, when
nights do not fall below 50 degrees

❧

When to Harvest
75 to 90 days after transplanting

❧

remove the plant and its potting mix from its container, and set them into the prepared hole so that the first set of true leaves is at the soil level. Fill the hole with soil, packing it gently around the roots. Pat down the surface and water to fill in any air pockets. ¶ Space plants 2 feet apart along walls, arbors, or trellises. As each plant grows, choose the side branches you want to develop to cover the structure. Pinch out unwanted side branches just above the first set of leaves. Tie the branches loosely to their support, and continue to pinch and prune to keep the shape you wish. Make sure to keep the soil moist but not soggy, and fertilize with a low-nitrogen liquid fertilizer every two weeks. Once the weather has warmed the ground, mulch each plant with 3 to 4 inches of organic compost in a circle 12 inches across.

Italian companions

From a culinary perspective, tomatoes come in either cooking (also called paste) or slicing types. When you cut open a long, meaty Roma or Milano, you will notice that there are only a few seed cavities and very thick walls. These meaty types cook down to a densely textured, intensely flavored sauce. The slicing varieties such as Early Girl and Hybrid Beefmaster have more cavities and thinner walls and, consequently, are better eaten raw than cooked. ¶ Everyone with just a bit of room in the tomato row should try to plant cooking varieties. All winter these can stamp a dish with quintessential tomato flavor, evoking the summer in their rich taste. See "About Cooking Tomatoes," page 75, for an easy way to freeze them. Hybridizers have developed varieties that mature early for cool-summer growers, but other types mature over a long season during the hot days of August. ¶ Once you have planted your tomatoes, ring them with basil, their perfect companion in the kitchen. ¶ **HOW TO DO IT** ¶ In the spring, after the last chance of frost, plant your tomatoes and basil. When tomato plants have three sets of true leaves, they are ready to set out. Make sure to harden them off for a week, by leaving them outside in a protected area during the day and bringing them inside at night. Before planting, submerge the transplants in their containers in a sink or bucket of water until air bubbles cease to appear. ¶ In prepared garden soil that is thoroughly moist, dig a hole for each tomato plant that is 8 inches wide and 8 inches deep or at least twice as wide and twice as deep as the container. Add ½ cup each bone meal and wood ashes to the bottom of the hole or follow the directions for a good-quality pelleted tomato food. For each basil plant, scoop out a hole 2 feet from a tomato plant that is twice as deep and wide as the root ball. ¶ As you prepare each hole, gently remove a tomato plant and its potting mix from its container, and ✒

Lycopersicon esculentum (tomato)
Ocimum basilicum (large-leaf basil)

What You Need
Tomato plants, bought or grown •
2 or more basil plants for each tomato plant • 6 or more square feet of prepared ground per set of plants • ½ cup each bone meal and wood ashes per tomato plant, or a good-quality pelleted tomato food • Stakes or wire cages • Low-nitrogen liquid fertilizer • Organic compost

Recommended Varieties
Cooking tomatoes: Costoluto Genovese, Milano, Paste Tomato, Principe Borghese, Roma, Royal Chico, San Marzano • Basil: any large-leaf Italian

Growing Conditions
¼ to a full day of direct sun

When to Buy
Seeds: in winter and spring from catalogues
Plants: in early spring from nurseries

When to Plant
Seeds: inside, 6 to 8 weeks before spring's last frost • Plants: after the last frost, when nights do not fall below 50 degrees

When to Harvest
Tomatoes: 63 to 82 days from transplanting • Basil: 75 days; snip off a few leaves when plants are 6 to 8 inches tall, about 55 days

set them in so that the first set of true leaves is at the soil level. Fill the hole with soil, packing it gently around the roots. Pat down the surface and water to fill in any air pockets. Plant the basil, setting the top of the root ball just at soil level. Fill the holes with potting mix and pat down the surface. Water to fill in air pockets. ¶ Add stakes alongside the tomato plants, or support them with wire cages. Keep the soil moist but not soggy, and fertilize tomatoes and basil with a low-nitrogen fertilizer every two weeks. When basil sends up flower stalks in late summer, cut them off to extend leaf production. Always let a few leaves remain on the plants. Once the weather has warmed the ground, mulch each plant with 3 to 4 inches of organic compost in a circle 12 inches across.

A TOWER OF BRIGHTLY COLORED TOMATOES

Gardeners who regretfully turn catalogue pages past the tomato section because they think their gardens are too small may have room after all. To optimize your planting, redesign your garden to incorporate vertical structures. ¶ **HOW TO DO IT** ¶ In the spring, after the last chance of frost, plant your tomatoes when plants have three sets of true leaves. Make sure to harden them off for a week by leaving them outside in a protected area during the day and bringing them inside at night. Before planting, submerge the transplants in their containers in a sink or bucket of water until air bubbles cease to appear. ¶ Draw a circle with a 4-foot diameter in a 5-foot square of prepared garden soil that is thoroughly moist. Select four 8-foot bamboo poles or wooden 1-by-2-inch stakes and space them vertically around the circumference. With wire, securely fasten the tops of the poles to make a teepee-shaped tower. ¶ At the outside edge of each stake, dig a hole that is 8 inches wide and 8 inches deep or at least twice as wide and twice as deep as one plant's container. Add ½ cup each bone meal and wood ashes to the bottom of the hole, or follow directions for a good-quality pelleted tomato food. ¶ Gently remove the plant and its potting mix from its container, and set them into the prepared hole so that the first set of true leaves is at the soil level. Fill the hole with soil, packing it gently around the roots. Pat down the surface and water to fill in any air pockets. Repeat at the other three corners. As the plants grow, tie them loosely to their stakes and train the branches inside the teepee. ¶ Keep the soil moist but not soggy, and fertilize with a low-nitrogen fertilizer every two weeks. Once the weather has warmed the ground, mulch each plant with 3 to 4 inches of organic compost in a circle 12 inches across.

Lycopersicon esculentum

❧

What You Need
4 tomato plants, bought or grown •
25 square feet of prepared ground •
4 bamboo or wooden stakes, 8 feet tall •
½ cup each bone meal and wood
ashes per plant, or a good-quality
pelleted tomato food •
Low-nitrogen liquid fertilizer •
Organic compost

❧

Recommended Varieties
Indeterminate cherry size: Green Grape,
Orange Cherry, Pink Pearl,
Red Pear, Ruby Pearl, Sweet 100,
Yellow Pear, Yellow Plum •
Indeterminate midsize: Early Girl, Golden
Jubilee, Lemon Boy,
Pink Girl, White Wonder

❧

Growing Conditions
¾ to a full day of direct sun

❧

When to Buy
Seeds: in winter and spring from catalogues
Plants: in early spring from nurseries

❧

When to Plant
Seeds: inside, 6 to 8 weeks before spring's
last frost • Plants: after the last frost, when
nights do not fall below 50 degrees

❧

When to Harvest
65 to 90 days after transplanting

❧

A SALSA GARDEN

Early in the 1990s there was revolutionary news in the food world: more salsa is being sold in America than ketchup. To make it fresh, plant complementary quantities of the ingredients to mature at the same time. ¶ The primary ingredients for salsa are tomatoes, peppers—either the tongue-tingling serrano or a milder jalapeño—and cilantro. Plant cilantro successively every three weeks. Let some plants go to seed, and by late season they will regrow on their own. ¶ **HOW TO DO IT** ¶ In the spring, after the last chance of frost, you can safely plant your tomatoes, peppers, and cilantro. When tomato plants have three sets of true leaves, they are ready to set out. Make sure to harden them off for a week by leaving them outside in a protected area during the day and bringing them inside at night. Before planting, submerge the transplants in their containers in a sink or bucket of water until air bubbles cease to appear. ¶ In prepared garden soil that is thoroughly moist, dig a hole for each tomato plant that is 8 inches wide and 8 inches deep or at least twice as wide and twice as deep as its container. Add ½ cup each bone meal and wood ashes to the bottom of the hole, or follow the directions for a good-quality pelleted tomato food. ¶ Gently remove the plant and its potting mix from its container, and set them into the prepared hole so that the first set of true leaves is at the soil level. Fill the hole with soil, packing it gently around the roots. Pat down the surface and water to fill in any air pockets. Add stakes or support the plants with wire cages. ¶ At least 4 feet away from the tomatoes, plant the chile peppers, keeping the root ball intact and just at soil level. Space the peppers 18 inches from ✦

Lycopersicon esculentum (*tomato*)
Capsicum (*chile peppers*)
Coriandrum sativum (*cilantro*)

❧

What You Need
Tomato plants, bought or grown, with maturation dates of 60 to 75 days • 2 chile pepper plants, with maturation dates of 60 to 75 days • 1 package of cilantro seeds • About 16 square feet of prepared ground per tomato with 2 pepper plants • ½ cup bone meal and wood ashes per tomato plant, or a good-quality pelleted tomato food • Stakes or wire cages • Low-nitrogen liquid fertilizer • Organic compost

❧

Recommended Varieties
Tomatoes: Celebrity, Early Girl, Early Pik Peppers: Early Jalapeño, Serrano Red Cilantro: Slo-bolt

❧

Growing Conditions
¾ to a full day of direct sun

❧

When to Buy
Seeds: in winter and spring from catalogues Plants: in early spring from nurseries

❧

When to Plant
Seeds: inside, 6 to 8 weeks before spring's last frost • Plants: after the last frost, when nights do not fall below 50 degrees

❧

When to Harvest
Tomatoes and chile peppers, 60 to 75 days after transplanting; start to use cilantro within one month of planting

❧

each other, without support. ¶ For cilantro, scatter the seeds over moist, prepared ground—to the east side of the tomatoes, so they will be shaded in the afternoon. Cover the seeds with ¼ inch of soil and pat down. As the seedlings grow, thin to 2 or 3 inches apart. ¶ Keep the soil moist but not soggy, and fertilize with a low-nitrogen fertilizer every two weeks. Once the weather has warmed the ground, mulch each tomato and pepper plant with 3 to 4 inches of organic compost in a circle 12 inches across.

GROWING

EXOTIC

VARIETIES

OF TOMATOES

A garden full of plump red tomatoes is a lovely sight, but a garden with a rainbow of colors and a diversity of shapes makes your daily picking like harvesting a treasure trove. If you marveled at last year's discovery of a tomato shiny-ripe when bright green, look at this year's new  champion in multicolored stripes. A sense of loyalty to that big red you have grown for any number of years can cause a struggle, but you can resolve it; grow just a couple of your old standards, and try out as many new ones as you have room for every year. ❧ Besides the fun and interest of trying something new, there is very good reason for you to experiment. New varieties are continually being developed that are more resistant to disease and insects, more productive, tastier, or tidier in size. ❧ Along with the wildly colored or rich-tasting tomatoes are some very close relatives that are a pleasure to add to your garden because they are cultivated just the same as tomatoes but have been largely ignored by home gardeners. Once you notice them in the catalogues, and sometimes in nurseries, you can add them to your garden and consequently to your pantry. ❧ When you try out something new, keep records to help you measure the performance. Write down when you planted, the varieties; the flavor, and the yield as well as any insect or disease problems you had. Your garden diary will help you plan an even better harvest next year.

TOMATILLO

This round green or sometimes purplish cousin of tomatoes comes wrapped in a pale green lacy husk, or calyx, that gradually dries and browns. There are gardeners who love the fruits but shake their heads at the wildly self-seeding habit that produces sprouts of the plant all over the garden. Still, tomatillos are easy to grow, and for devotees of Hispanic cooking they are an invaluable member of the culinary garden with their tart, slightly citrusy flavor. Three plants give a generous harvest. Make sure that the husk has cracked before picking. ¶ **HOW TO DO IT** ¶ In the spring, after the last chance of frost, you can safely plant your tomatillos. When plants have three sets of true leaves, they are ready to set out. Before planting, submerge the transplants in their containers in a sink or bucket of water until air bubbles cease to appear. ¶ In prepared garden soil that is thoroughly moist, dig a hole for each plant that is 8 inches wide and 8 inches deep or at least twice as wide and twice as deep as its container. Add to the bottom of the hole ½ cup each bone meal and wood ashes per plant, or follow the directions for a good-quality pelleted tomato food. ¶ Gently remove the plant and its potting mix from its container, and set them into the prepared hole so that the first set of true leaves is at the soil level. Fill the hole with soil, packing it gently around the roots. Pat down the surface and water to fill in any air pockets. ¶ Space plants 2 feet apart or tuck them between caged tomatoes that are spaced 3 to 4 feet apart. The husks keep tomatillos that sprawl from rotting, but if you prefer, set up wire cages, stakes, or other support at the time of planting. Keep the soil moist, but not soggy, and fertilize with a low-nitrogen fertilizer every two weeks. Once the weather has warmed the ground, mulch each plant with 3 to 4 inches of organic compost in a circle 12 inches across.

Physalis ixocarpa (*tomatillo*)

What You Need
*Tomatillo plants, bought or grown•
About 6 square feet of prepared ground per plant•
½ cup each bone meal and wood ashes per plant, or a good-quality pelleted tomato food•
Low-nitrogen liquid fertilizer•
Organic compost*

Recommended Varieties
Any available

Growing Conditions
¾ of a day of direct sun

When to Buy
*Seeds: in winter and spring from catalogues
Plants: in early spring from nurseries*

When to Plant
Seeds: inside, 6 weeks before spring's last frost•Plants: after the last frost, when nights do not fall below 50 degrees

When to Harvest
75 days from transplanting

FRENCH IMPORTS

The French are passionate about their food, gathering the freshest ingredients from their kitchen gardens. Whatever is not growing fresh there the French home cook can purchase in the weekly or daily markets, where the variety is staggering. Stands are piled high with a dozen varieties of tomatoes, pyramids of peaches, baskets of four kinds of cherries, and barrels of olives mixed with herbs and flavored with lemons or kumquats. The concern with intense flavors and silky textures has led the French to preserve the very best varieties of fruits and vegetables, which some American catalogues now feature. ¶ **HOW TO DO IT** ¶ In the spring, after the last chance of frost, you can safely plant your tomatoes. When plants have three sets of true leaves they are ready to set out. Make sure to harden them off for a week by leaving them outside in a protected area during the day and bringing them inside at night. Before planting, submerge the transplants in their containers in a sink or bucket of water until air bubbles cease to appear. ¶ In prepared garden soil that is thoroughly moist, dig a hole for each plant that is 8 inches wide and 8 inches deep or at least twice as wide and twice as deep as its container. Add ½ cup each bone meal and wood ashes to the bottom of the hole, or follow the directions for a good-quality pelleted tomato food. ¶ Gently remove the plant and its potting mix from its container, and set them into the prepared hole so that the first set of true leaves is at the soil level. Fill the hole with soil, packing it gently around the roots. Pat down the surface and water to fill in any air pockets. Set up wire cages, stakes, or other support. ¶ Keep the soil moist but not soggy, and fertilize with a low-nitrogen fertilizer every two weeks. Once the weather has warmed the ground, mulch each plant with 3 to 4 inches of organic compost in a circle 12 inches across.

Lycopersicon esculentum

What You Need
Tomato plants, bought or grown, of French varieties.
About 6 square feet of prepared ground per plant.
½ cup each bone meal and wood ashes per plant, or a good-quality pelleted tomato food.
Stakes or wire cages.
Low-nitrogen liquid fertilizer.
Organic compost

Recommended Varieties
Carmello, Cobra, Dona, Lorissa, Marmande, Salsa

Growing Conditions
¼ to a full day of direct sun

When to Buy
Seeds: in winter and spring from catalogues
Plants: in early spring from nurseries

When to Plant
Seeds: inside, 6 to 8 weeks before spring's last frost. Plants: after the last frost, when nights do not fall below 50 degrees

When to Harvest
Carmello, 70 days after transplanting. Cobra, 74 days. Dona, 65 days. Lorissa, 72 days. Marmande, 73 days. Salsa, 72 days

STUFFING TOMATOES

Thick-walled, bulky-shaped stuffing tomatoes make up for their very mild flavor by their usefulness. Bake them overflowing with vegetables and topped with bread crumbs. Use them to serve sauces and cold soup, or pack salads in them for picnics. ¶ There are determinate varieties of stuffing tomatoes, so you can grow these in containers, but remember to plant them for successive harvest. Most of the varieties are mid or late season, so if you live in a cool climate, get them into the ground as soon as you can in order to produce a harvest. ¶ **HOW TO DO IT** ¶ In the spring, after the last chance of frost, plant your tomatoes when plants have three sets of true leaves. Make sure to harden them off for a week by leaving them outside in a protected area during the day and bringing them inside at night. Before planting, submerge the transplants in their containers in a sink or bucket of water until air bubbles cease to appear. ¶ In prepared garden soil that is thoroughly moist, dig a hole for each plant that is 8 inches wide and 8 inches deep or at least twice as wide and twice as deep as the container. Add ½ cup each bone meal and wood ashes to the bottom of the hole, or follow the directions for a good-quality pelleted tomato food. ¶ Gently remove the plant and its potting mix from its container, and set them into the prepared hole so that the first set of true leaves is at the soil level. Fill the hole with soil, packing it gently around the roots. Pat down the surface and water to fill in any air pockets. Space the determinate varieties a little closer than indeterminates, about 18 inches apart. Set up wire cages, stakes, or other support. ¶ Keep the soil moist but not soggy, and fertilize with a low-nitrogen fertilizer every two weeks. Once the weather has warmed the ground, mulch each plant with 3 to 4 inches of organic compost in a circle 12 inches across.

Lycopersicon esculentum

What You Need
Tomato plants, bought or grown •
About 6 square feet of prepared ground per plant •
½ cup each bone meal and wood ashes per plant, or a good-quality pelleted tomato food •
Stakes or wire cages •
Low-nitrogen liquid fertilizer •
Organic compost

Recommended Varieties
Burgess Stuffing Tomato, Dad's Mug, Ruffled Tomato, Yellow Stuffer

Growing Conditions
¾ to a full day of direct sun

When to Buy
Seeds: in winter and spring from catalogues
Plants: in early spring from nurseries

When to Plant
Seeds: inside, 6 to 8 weeks before spring's last frost • Plants: after the last frost, when nights do not fall below 50 degrees

When to Harvest
Burgess Stuffing Tomato, 65 to 70 days after transplanting • Dad's Mug, 85 to 95 days • Ruffled Tomato, 68 days • Yellow Stuffer, 75 days

GROUND CHERRIES

Ground cherries are distant cousins of tomatoes, with cherry-sized golden fruits encased in a papery husk like a tomatillo. There may be a family resemblance, but it does not carry over to taste, for the flavor of ground cherries is rich, tart, sweet, and herbal. The seeds are available in catalogues, but they are often listed under names like Gooseberry Strawberry, Husk Tomato, or Poha Berry. ¶ The Italians have raised these little gems for years, serving them for a fruit course with the husks pulled back over the shoulders like wings. Their rich taste with citrus flavors makes them right for tarts and pies if you can resist eating them fresh with just the warmth of the sun for seasoning. ¶ **HOW TO DO IT** ¶ In the spring, after the last chance of frost, you can safely plant your ground cherries. When plants have three sets of true leaves, they are ready to set out. Before planting, submerge the transplants in their containers in a sink or bucket of water until air bubbles cease to appear. ¶ In prepared garden soil that is thoroughly moist, dig a hole for each plant that is 8 inches wide and 8 inches deep or at least twice as wide and twice as deep as the container. Add ½ cup each bone meal and wood ashes to the bottom of the hole, or follow the directions for a good-quality pelleted tomato food. ¶ Gently remove the plant and its potting mix from its container, and set them into the prepared hole so that the first set of true leaves is at the soil level. Fill the hole with soil, packing it gently around the roots. Pat down the surface and water to fill in any air pockets. Let the plants sprawl or, if you prefer, set up wire cages, stakes, or other support. ¶ Keep the soil moist but not soggy, and fertilize with a low-nitrogen fertilizer every two weeks. Once the weather has warmed the ground, mulch each plant with 3 to 4 inches of organic compost in a circle 12 inches across.

Physalis peruviana (*ground cherry*)

What You Need
Ground cherry plants, bought or grown •
About 6 square feet of prepared ground per plant •
½ cup each bone meal and wood ashes per plant, or a good-quality pelleted tomato food •
Stakes or wire cages •
Low-nitrogen liquid fertilizer •
Organic compost

Recommended Varieties
Any available

Growing Conditions
¾ of a day of direct sun

When to Buy
Seeds: in winter and spring from catalogues
Plants: in early spring from nurseries

When to Plant
Seeds: inside, 6 to 8 weeks before spring's last frosts • Plants: after the last frost, when nights do not fall below 50 degrees

When to Harvest
70 days for the first ripe fruits; about 100 days for good yields

OLD-FASHIONED FAVORITES

The seed companies that now are reintroducing older tomato varieties, which are unwaveringly flavorful, call them heirloom, old-fashioned, or open-pollinated. Breeders have lately improved the resistance of some varieties, and catalogues specify the hardier types. If you have soil diseases you might try growing the old-fashioned varieties in containers with purchased potting mix. Try them for their enhanced flavor, and enjoy their funny looks so unlike the well-bred, perfectly round tomato. ¶ **HOW TO DO IT** ¶

In the spring, after the last chance of frost, you can begin to plant your tomatoes. When plants have three sets of true leaves, they are ready to set out. Make sure to harden them off for a week by leaving them outside in a protected area during the day and bringing them inside at night. Before planting, submerge the transplants in their containers in a sink or bucket of water until air bubbles cease to appear. ¶ In prepared garden soil that is thoroughly moist, dig a hole for each plant that is 8 inches wide and 8 inches deep or at least twice as deep and twice as wide as the container. Add ½ cup each bone meal and wood ashes to the bottom of the hole, or follow the directions for a good-quality pelleted tomato food. ¶ Gently remove the plant and its potting mix from its container, and set them into the prepared hole so that the first set of true leaves is at the soil level. Fill the hole with soil, packing it gently around the roots. Pat down the surface and water to fill in any air pockets. Set up wire cages, stakes, or other support. ¶ Keep the soil moist but not soggy, and fertilize with a low-nitrogen fertilizer every two weeks. Once the weather has warmed the ground, mulch each plant with 3 to 4 inches of organic compost in a circle 12 inches across.

Lycopersicon esculentum

What You Need
Tomato plants, bought or grown • About 6 square feet of prepared ground per plant • Stakes or wire cages • ½ cup each bone meal and wood ashes per plant, or a good-quality pelleted tomato food • Low-nitrogen liquid fertilizer • Organic compost

Recommended Varieties
Brandywine, Costoluto Genovese, Golden Pearl, Great White, Mortgage Lifter, Old Flame

Growing Conditions
¾ to a full day of direct sun

When to Buy
Seeds: in winter and spring from catalogues
Plants: in early spring from nurseries

When to Plant
Seeds: inside, six weeks before spring's last frost • Plants: after the last frost, when nights do not fall below 50 degrees

When to Harvest
Brandywine, 95 days after transplanting • Costoluto Genovese, 78 • Golden Pearl, 67 • Great White, 85 • Mortgage Lifter, 85 • Old Flame, 80

Beefsteak tomatoes

By reputation beefsteak tomatoes are the most American of any, an integral part of the Labor Day picnic table, covering in one slice an extra-large hamburger bun. It may seem peculiar to introduce them as a new exotic breed, but of all the myths and mystiques in the tomato world, that of growing the platter-sized two-pound beefsteak may be the most common. ¶ With the incredible press and stardom of the beefsteak, gardeners all over America have been trying for years to grow them, but up to now the actuality has been that beefsteaks are inconstant and difficult, not as ubiquitously successful as the tomato-vine rumor would have it. Gardeners have been blaming their skill for fruit that is mild flavored, coarse textured, and generally insipid. In fact, they were growing fickle varieties specialized for eccentric climates. ¶ Now that is all about to change. If you want to grow the breeders' new beefsteaks yourself, you must have good hot summer temperatures and a long growing season, because beefsteaks are a late-season variety, but the delicate balance of heat, humidity, and night temperature is no longer as important. ¶ The fruits are so large, and so heavy, make sure to grow beefsteaks in concrete-reinforcing-wire cages to ensure plenty of support for them and for the plants. Space the cages apart generously to keep the plants from shading one another and supply as much sunlight and heat as possible. ¶ **HOW TO DO IT** ¶ In the spring, after the last chance of frost, you can safely plant your tomatoes. When plants have three sets of true leaves, they are ready to set out. Make sure to harden them off for a week by leaving them outside in a protected area during the day and bringing them inside at night. Before planting, submerge the transplants in their containers in a sink or bucket of water until air bubbles cease to appear. ¶ In prepared garden soil that is thoroughly moist, dig a ✐

Lycopersicon esculentum

❧

What You Need

Tomato plants, bought or grown •
About 12 square feet of
prepared ground per plant •
½ cup each bone meal and wood ashes
per plant, or a good-quality
pelleted tomato food •
Concrete-reinforcing-wire cages 4-feet high
with a 2-foot diameter •
Low-nitrogen liquid fertilizer •
Organic compost

❧

Recommended Varieties

Bragger, Brandywine, Burpee's Supersteak
VFN Hybrid, Hybrid Beefmaster, Large

❧

Growing Conditions

¼ to a full day of direct sun

❧

When to Buy

Seeds: in winter and spring from catalogues
Plants: in early spring from nurseries

❧

When to Plant

Seeds: inside, 6 to 8 weeks before spring's
last frost • Plants: after the last frost, when
nights do not fall below 50 degrees

❧

When to Harvest

Bragger, 80 days after transplanting •
Brandywine, 90 days • Burpee's Supersteak
VFN Hybrid, 80 days • Hybrid
Beefmaster, 80 days • Large, 110 days

❧

hole for each plant that is 8 inches wide and 8 inches deep or at least twice as wide and twice as deep as its container. Add ½ cup each bone meal and wood ashes to the bottom of the hole, or follow the directions for a good-quality pelleted tomato food. ¶ Gently remove the plant and its potting mix from its container, and set them into the prepared hole so that the first set of true leaves is at the soil level. Fill the hole with soil, packing it gently around the roots. Pat down the surface and water to fill in any air pockets. Space plants 4 feet apart, and set up wire cages; beefsteaks need sturdy support. ¶ Keep the soil moist, but not soggy, and fertilize with a low-nitrogen fertilizer every two weeks. Once the weather has warmed the ground, mulch each plant with 3 to 4 inches of organic compost in a circle 12 inches across.

FRESH

TOMATOES

IN THE

KITCHEN

Cooking with garden-sweet, fresh tomatoes if you are used to chopping up the supermarket variety is like learning how to use a totally new ingredient. If cooking green tomatoes is new to you, try pickling excess green cherry tomatoes, and fry up any of the larger green fruit that are left when you pull up the vines. ❧ To protect fresh tomatoes' sweetness once you take them off the vine, never refrigerate them. The cold changes their sugars to starch, ruining their taste. For longer storage, if a harvest of paste tomatoes is more than you can cook, freeze these meaty varieties to make sauces or stews. Simply wash and dry them and then toss them whole into the freezer. When frozen solid, store in air-proof plastic freezer bags. Give away garden-fresh slicing tomatoes rather than trying to store them. ❧ Many

great arguments have contributed to the peel-or-not-peel tomato controversy. Diehards leave peels on, but the daintier sort prefer to pop their tomatoes into boiling water for thirty seconds, then into an ice bath. This variation on Finnish sauna treatment causes the peel to slide off easily. ❧ Another skin-loosening method is to grill tomatoes until the skins are blackened. You can use the flame of a gas burner or your barbecue. Let the tomatoes become quite black, the skin cracked and blistered with the heat. Once peeled the tomatoes retain a smoky flavor, which underpins cooked sauces and fresh salsas. ❧ Diehards also leave the seeds in, but after long cooking the seeds of the tomato give off a bitter quality. To seed tomatoes, cut them in half crosswise. Hold the tomato halves upside down, and gently squeeze and shake them until the seeds fall out. ❧ Cooking the multitude of tomato varieties is an adventure, but remember to keep your perspective. Any single tomato picked off the bush, dusted clean, and popped straight into your mouth is just about as good as it gets.

Dried tomatoes in olive oil

The height in popularity of dried tomatoes is matched only by the sky-high prices they fetch on supermarket shelves, but you can easily prepare them yourself. Any variety of tomato can be dried, but the meatier, paste types result in a more substantial dried piece than the thinner-textured, slicing varieties. Experiment with all the varieties you grow, because what you gain in dried weight from a paste tomato you lose in flavor compared to the sweeter, more intense, juicy slicing varieties. Many people prefer the little disks that cherry tomatoes make when dried because they soften easier and can be used whole on pizzas and in pasta. ¶ Start by cutting your tomatoes in half and lightly salting them on both sides. If you prefer to use an electric dehydrator, follow the directions that come with the machine. Otherwise, spread them on baking sheets or screens, cover them loosely with cheesecloth or clear plastic wrap, and place them in the sun. Bring in the tomatoes every night before the evening dew can settle on them, and turn them at least once a day until they are leathery without any moist spots. Do not overdry the tomatoes or you will lose both flavor and texture. ¶ Store your dried tomatoes in an air-tight package on the shelf, or add them to good-quality, fruity-tasting virgin olive oil (not an extra virgin with its own intense flavor), as described. ¶ **HOW TO DO IT** ¶ Drop the dried tomatoes into a medium-sized saucepan filled with boiling water. Boil the tomatoes for two minutes and remove them immediately. Drain them on paper toweling.¶ Add the tomatoes, rosemary, and optionally the garlic clove to a large, clean, dry quart glass jar with a large mouth and a lid. Pour in the olive oil to cover the tomatoes, which will expand. Seal the jar and store it in the refrigerator, adding more oil to keep the tomatoes covered. The oil will solidify in the refrigerator, but left at room temperature it will return to normal consistency. ¶ Beginning after ten days, taste the oil by pouring it on a ✒

Dried Tomatoes in Olive Oil
❧
What You Need
2 cups dried tomatoes •
1 sprig rosemary •
1 garlic clove (optional) •
Fruity olive oil (not extra virgin)
❧

little piece of bread. When you find the flavor of rosemary strong enough, remove it and the garlic to avoid their spoiling the oil. Store the jar in a cool dark place. It will keep for several months. ¶ Note: If you wish, you can blend some of the olive oil and tomatoes in a food processor to make a pumate, a dried-tomato spread delicious on crackers or toasts. Also drizzle the oil over pizza, dot it on soups, or toss salads with it. ¶ Makes about 1 quart.

Garden-grown tomato salads

These salads are sublime made with your freshest, sweetest tomatoes. The intense colors of the fruit at their peak highlight the extravagances of the tomato harvest. ¶ **PANZANELLA** ¶ *Shreds of basil, a grind of pepper, and a toss of salt bring out tomatoes' juices and flavors. Sweet and fragrant, this is the memorable dish you will yearn for when winter snows cover the tomato patch and warm summer picnics seem very long off.* ¶ **HOW TO DO IT** ¶ In a large salad bowl, mix together the basil, olive oil, vinegar, garlic, and salt and pepper. Add the tomatoes and toss very gently. Then add the bread cubes and toss again gently. Let the salad sit for ten minutes to allow the bread to absorb the sweet tomato juices. Mix again and serve at once. Serves 6. ¶ **MORE-THAN-JUST-RED TOMATO SALAD, WITH PARSLEY VINAIGRETTE** ¶ *This salad only gets better as it marinates in the vinaigrette. Leftovers can be made into tomato sandwiches the next day, if there are any leftovers.* ¶ **HOW TO DO IT** ¶ Place the sliced tomatoes on a platter and lightly salt and pepper them on both sides. ¶ Place ½ cup olive oil and the garlic, bread crumbs, mustard, vinegar, and optionally the anchovies in the container of a food processor or blender. Process at high speed for one minute or until the garlic and bread crumbs are well blended. Then, while the machine is running, gradually add the parsley. Continue to process until the parsley has been chopped fine. Add the rest of the oil and process for one more minute. ¶ Pour the sauce over the tomatoes. Toss gently. Let the flavors marinate for thirty minutes, and serve at room temperature. ¶ Serves 4 to 6.

Panzanella

What You Need
3 tablespoons fine shreds of basil •
4 tablespoons virgin olive oil •
2 tablespoons balsamic vinegar •
1 clove garlic, finely chopped •
Salt and freshly ground pepper to taste •
8 cups 1-inch pieces of tomatoes •
2 cups cubed day-old Italian bread

More-Than-Just-Red Tomato Salad, with Parsley Vinaigrette

What You Need
4 red tomatoes, sliced •
3 yellow tomatoes, sliced •
1 cup red cherry tomatoes, sliced •
1 cup small yellow plum tomatoes, sliced •
Salt and freshly ground pepper to taste

For Parsley Vinaigrette:
1 cup olive oil •
1 clove garlic •
2 tablespoons white bread crumbs •
1 teaspoon Dijon-style mustard •
4 tablespoons red wine vinegar •
2 anchovies (optional) •
1 cup fresh curly parsley leaves •
1 cup Italian parsley leaves •
Salt and freshly ground pepper to taste

ROASTED TOMATO SOUP

Summer is the time for simplicity, because the intensely rich flavors of the food grown fresh need no mask. This rustic soup makes the very best use of the tomatoes you have grown, with the fragrance of rosemary just as it wafts through the garden when the summer sun warms its leaves in the air. ¶ **HOW TO DO IT** ¶ Preheat the oven to 450 degrees F. ¶ Coat the bottom of a large roasting pan with the olive oil. Place the tomatoes and the onions in the pan and rub them with the oil. Roast them for forty-five minutes to one hour, or until the tomatoes are beginning to split and collapse and the onions are golden brown and cooked all the way through. ¶ Place the tomatoes and onions in a food processor or blender with 1 cup of the chicken stock, and process until smooth. If you prefer a very smooth-textured soup, put the mixture through a food mill or sieve at this point. Transfer the contents to a saucepan and pour in the remaining chicken stock. ¶ Add the rosemary sprigs and heat the soup gently, until almost boiling. Remove the rosemary, add salt and pepper, and serve. ¶ Serves 4 to 6 as a first course.

What You Need
4 tablespoons olive oil •
8 medium tomatoes, left whole •
4 small yellow onions, quartered •
3 cups chicken stock •
2 sprigs rosemary •
Salt and freshly ground pepper to taste

Stylish summer salsas

Either tomatillos or tomatoes make a base for a refreshingly tart salsa that is delicious dipped up with corn chips, spread as a surprising "pickle" relish on summer hamburgers, or offered as a sophisticated fresh sauce to take the place of lemon seasoning on fish. For a cold pasta salad, double the Green Salsa or use Salsa Fresca to dress a pound of dried pasta that you have cooked, tossed with a little oil, and allowed to cool. Innumerable variations to either salsa include additions of fresh corn kernels, chopped green or red peppers, and chopped avocados according to your taste.

¶ **GREEN SALSA** ¶ *Do not be surprised to discover that tomatillos are characteristically sticky under their pale coats of husk. Wash them lightly and dry before using.* ¶ **HOW TO DO IT** ¶ Combine all the ingredients in the bowl of a food processor. Chop for one minute or until all ingredients are chopped coarsely, not ground, and are blended. ¶ Use immediately or store covered in the refrigerator for up to four days. Makes 2 cups. ¶ **SALSA FRESCA** ¶ *This salsa varies from the usual in its use of basil and mint, which give it a refreshing zing without a spicy nip.* ¶ **HOW TO DO IT** ¶ Mix together all the ingredients for the salsa, and toss well. ¶ Serve immediately. Makes 3 cups.

Green Salsa

❧

What You Need

1 pound tomatillos, roughly chopped •
½ cup chopped white onions •
2 cloves garlic, chopped •
2 jalapeño chilies, seeded and
coarsely chopped •
1 cup coarsely chopped cilantro leaves •
Juice of 1 lime •
Salt to taste

❧

Salsa Fresca

❧

What You Need

3 ripe red tomatoes, coarsely chopped •
3 ripe yellow tomatoes, coarsely chopped •
1 cup cherry tomatoes, cut in halves •
¼ cup finely chopped fresh basil •
3 tablespoons finely chopped fresh mint •
1 garlic clove, finely chopped •
2 green onions, finely chopped •
1 teaspoon fresh lemon juice •
Salt and freshly ground pepper to taste

❧

GREEN TOMATOES, FRIED OR PICKLED

Before the film Fried Green Tomatoes at the Whistle Stop Cafe, *not many people outside the South knew that unripe tomatoes were useful in the kitchen, to cook with, to pickle, and to substitute for green apples in pies and chutneys. Green tomatoes are tart but without the distinctive taste of vine-ripened fruits. This makes them perfect for a variety of recipes that jazz up their flavor and make use of their crunchy flesh. Green tomatoes hold their shape when fried and their crispness when pickled.*

¶ **FRIED GREEN TOMATOES IN AN HERB CRUST** ¶ *Green tomatoes are a classic dish in old-fashioned, friendly Southern cooking even if they achieved stardom only with the film. There are now varieties of green tomatoes that stay bright green when they are sweet and ripe, so do not confuse these with the unripe tomatoes called for here. Try poached eggs dolloped with salsa on top of the crisped tomato slices for breakfast, or pair them with a simple entrée off the grill.* ¶**HOW TO DO IT** ¶ Place the tomatoes on a plate and lightly salt and pepper them on both sides. Let them sit while you prepare the cornmeal crust. ¶ Toss all the rest of the ingredients except the olive oil together in a medium-sized bowl. One by one, place each slice of tomato in the bowl and turn to coat both sides with the cornmeal crust. ¶ In a medium-sized sauté pan, heat the olive oil over moderate heat. Cook the crusted tomatoes on both sides until they are golden brown and beginning to soften. Drain on paper towels and serve at once. Serves 4 to 6. ¶ **GREEN MARBLE PICKLES** ¶ These tomato pickles are the easiest way to save garden bounty. Picking some cherry tomatoes while they are green helps keep your harvest under control. Vary the pickles by adding fresh beans, snap peas, ✒

Fried Green Tomatoes
in an Herb Crust
❧

What You Need

4 green tomatoes, sliced ¼-inch thick •
Salt and freshly ground pepper to taste •
1 cup cornmeal •
1 teaspoon salt •
1 tablespoon finely chopped
fresh sage leaves •
1 tablespoon finely chopped parsley leaves •
1 tablespoon finely chopped
fresh thyme leaves •
2 tablespoons finely chopped onion •
2 tablespoons olive oil
❧

Green Marble Pickles
❧

What You Need

2 cups green cherry tomatoes, left whole •
1 cup small pickling onions,
peeled and left whole •
2 cloves garlic •
1 slice of carrot •
1 large sprig fresh dill or
2 tablespoons dried dill seed •
1 cup white vinegar •
1 cup water •
1 tablespoon sea salt •
1 tablespoon sugar •
1 tablespoon mustard seeds •
1 bay leaf •
1 small dried pepper or 1 teaspoon
pepper flakes
❧

green onions, or baby carrots. If martinis are your summer delight, substitute one of these pickles for your traditional olive; of course, the pickled onions are delicious as well. ¶ **HOW TO DO IT** ¶ Thoroughly wash a quart jar, and rinse it with very hot water. Pack the jar with the tomatoes, onions, carrot slice, garlic, and fresh dill. ¶ Heat together the vinegar, water, salt, sugar, mustard seeds, bay leaf, and dried pepper in a saucepan over high heat. When the brine comes to a boil, pour it into the jar, seal, and store in the refrigerator. The pickles are ready to eat after two weeks, but if you can wait, they are even more delicious after one month. ¶ Makes 1 quart.

EXPANDED LIST OF FAVORITE TOMATOES

Of the innumerable varieties of tomatoes available for the home garden as both seeds and young plants, some are classics, some are special purpose, and some are only briefly stylish. Here is a limited selection of some current favorites chosen for flavor and dependability, and also for interest. Experiment every year with those that especially intrigue you, for a harvest that expands your repertoire as well as indulging your palate.

Basket King Hybrid: determinate midsize, red; midseason

Better Boy: indeterminate large, red; midseason

Bragger: indeterminate beefsteak, red; midseason

Brandywine: indeterminate beefsteak, deep wine red, intense flavor; late season

Burgess Stuffing Tomato: determinate stuffing, red; midseason

Burpee's Pixie Hybrid: determinate large cherry, red; late season

Burpee's Supersteak Hybrid: indeterminate beefsteak, red; midseason

Carmello: indeterminate midsize, red, one of the tasty French varieties; midseason

Celebrity: determinate midsize, red, reliable producer; midseason

Chello Hybrid: semideterminate cherry, yellow; early season

Climbing Trip-L Crop: indeterminate large, red; late season

Cobra: indeterminate large, red, one of the tasty French varieties; midseason

Costoluto Genovese: indeterminate cooking, red; late season

Dad's Mug: indeterminate stuffing, pink red; late season

Dona: indeterminate midsize, red, one of the tasty French varieties; early season

Early Cascade: indeterminate large cherry, red; early season

Early Cherry: determinate cherry, red; early season

Early Girl: indeterminate midsize, red; for many, the most reliable in all areas; early season

Early Pik: determinate midsize, red; extra-early season

Floragold Basket: determinate cherry, yellow; late season

Giant Tree: indeterminate large, red; late season

Gold Nugget: determinate cherry, yellow; midseason

Golden Jubilee: indeterminate midsize, golden yellow; late season

Golden Pearl: indeterminate cherry, yellow; early season

Great White: indeterminate beefsteak, white; late season

Green Grape: determinate cherry, yellow-green color when ripe; midseason

Husky Cherry Red: dwarf indeterminate cherry, red; midseason

Husky Gold: dwarf indeterminate midsize, yellow; midseason

Husky Pink: dwarf indeterminate midsize, pink; midseason

Hybrid Beefmaster: indeterminate beefsteak, red; late season

Large: indeterminate beefsteak, red; late season

Lemon Boy: indeterminate midsize, yellow; midseason

Lorissa: indeterminate midsize, red, one of the tasty French varieties; midseason

Marmande: semideterminate large, red, one of the tasty French varieties; midseason

Milano: indeterminate cooking, red; late season

Mortgage Lifter: indeterminate beefsteak, pink, old-fashioned variety; late season

Old Flame: indeterminate large, red, old-fashioned variety; late season

Orange Cherry: indeterminate cherry, orange; midseason

Orange Pixie: determinate large cherry, orange; extra-early season

Oregon Spring: determinate midsize, red, very early type; extra-early type

Oregon Star: indeterminate beefsteak, red, early-beefsteak type; early season

Park's Whopper: indeterminate beefsteak, red; late season

Paste Tomato: determinate cooking, red; late season

Pink Girl: indeterminate midsize, pink; midseason

Pink Pearl: indeterminate cherry, pink; midseason

Principe Burghese: determinate cherry, cooking, excellent for drying; midseason

Red Cherry: indeterminate cherry, red; midseason

Red Pear: indeterminate pear-shaped cherry, red; midseason

Roma: determinate cooking, red; midseason

Royal Chico: determinate cooking, red; midseason

Ruby Pearl: indeterminate cherry, pinky red; midseason

Ruffled Tomato: indeterminate stuffing, yellow; midseason

Salsa: semideterminate midsize, red; midseason

San Marzano: indeterminate cooking, red; late season

Small Fry: determinate cherry, red, excellent for hanging baskets; early season

Solar Set: determinate large, red, excellent for high temperatures; midseason

Stupice: indeterminate midsize, red, very early type; extra-early season

Sub Artic: determinate large cherry, red, very early type; extra-early season

Superb Super Bush: determinate midsize, red; late season

Supersweet 100/Sweet 100: indeterminate cherry, red; early season

VFN Hybrid Beefmaster: indeterminate beefsteak, red; late season

White Wonder: indeterminate midsize, white; late season

Yellow Pear: indeterminate pear-shaped cherry, yellow; late season

Yellow Plum: indeterminate egg-shaped cherry, yellow; midseason

Yellow Stuffer: indeterminate cooking, yellow; midseason

Seed and plant sources

Most companies grow and test their seeds before they sell them. Although they offer seeds to grow in gardens all over America, they know what grows well in their area. Call the companies closest to your location if you need suggestions about tomatoes that will grow in your climate. Some companies charge for their catalogue. Call first to check prices and availability.

Bountiful Gardens
18001 Shafer Ranch Road
Willits, CA 95490
707 459-6410
Seeds, garden craft items, tools, and supplies.

W. Atlee Burpee & Co.
PO Box 5114
Warminster, PA 18974
215 674-9633
Seeds only. An all-purpose catalogue with a standard selection of seeds.

Foxhill Farm
443 West Michigan Avenue
PO Box 9
Parma, MI 49269
517 531-3179
Fax 513 531-3179
Plants year-round. Many varieties of basils and rosemaries.

Heirloom Garden Seeds
PO Box 138
Guerneville, CA 95446
707 869-0967
Seeds only. This catalogue features heirloom and old-fashioned nonhybrid seeds and offers ten different varieties of basil.

Johnny's Selected Seeds
310 Foss Hill Road
Albion, ME 04910
207 437-9294
Seeds for tomatillo and ground (husk) cherry, and five different types of basil.

Native Seeds
2509 North Campbell Avenue, #325
Tucson, AZ 85719
Seeds of tomatillos.

Nichols Garden Nursery
1190 North Pacific Highway
Albany, OR 97321
503 928-9280
A good selection of tomato seeds, and seeds and plants of herbs (herb plants shipped only in spring and fall).

Ornamental Edibles
3622 Weedin Court
San Jose, CA 95132
408 946-SEED
Thirty varieties of tomatoes, plus unusual vegetable and herb seeds. Look for Banana Legs, bearing clusters of yellow tomatoes that are banana shaped, crunchy, and sweet. Also offers a number of French varieties.

Pinetree Garden Seeds
Route 100
New Gloucester, ME 04260
207 926-3400
Tomatoes in 45 different varieties. Look for Prudence Purple, an early, full-sized, purplish-skinned tomato that has a great flavor and is very disease resistant for an old-fashioned variety.

Redwood City Seed Company
PO Box 361
Redwood City, CA 94064
415 325-7333
Seeds only, featuring unusual varieties of herbs and tomatoes from all over the world.

Seeds of Change
1364 Rufina Circle #5
Santa Fe, NM 87501
505 438-8080
Organic seeds and 65 varieties of heirloom and hybrid tomato varieties, including Canner's Delight, Double Rich, Golden Jubilee, Marble Stripe, Orange Queen, Oregon Spring Bush.

Shepherd's Garden Seeds
6116 Highway 9
Felton, CA 95018
408 335-5216
Fax 408 335-2080
Quality seeds featuring international varieties of unusually fine taste, including a number of the French varieties.

Territorial Seed Co.
PO Box 157
Cottage Grove, OR 97424
503 942-9547
An extensive list of early-season tomato varieties
for cool summer climates, plus over 400 varieties
of other specialty seeds.

The Cook's Garden
PO Box 535
Londonderry, VT 05148
802 824-3400
Fax 802 824-3027
Nine types of basil, many annual and perennial
herbs, and excellent tomato varieties.

Tomato Growers Supply Company
PO Box 2237
Fort Myers, CA 33902
813 768-1119
Unusual heirloom and hybrid varieties of toma-
toes. Also a source for seeds of tomatoes to grow in
Southern climates.

Bibliography

Behr, Edward.
The Artful Eater.
New York: Atlantic Monthly Press, 1992.

Brennan, Georgeanne, and
Mimi Luebbermann.
Little Herb Gardens.
San Francisco: Chronicle Books, 1993.

Brennan, Georgeanne.
*Potager: Fresh Garden Cooking
in the French Style.*
San Francisco: Chronicle Books, 1992.

Coleman, Eliot.
*The New Organic Grower's Four Season
Harvest.*
Post Mills, Vermont: Chelsey Green
Publishing Company, 1992.

Creasy, Rosalind.
Cooking from the Garden.
San Francisco: Sierra Club Books, 1988.

Doty, Walter A., and A. Cort Sinnes.
All About Tomatoes.
San Francisco: Ortho Books, 1981.

Gershuny, Grace, and
Deborah L. Martin.
The Rodale Book of Composting.
Emmaus, Pennsylvania: Rodale
Publishing, 1992

Hortus Third Dictionary.
New York: MacMillan, 1976.

Lima, Patrick.
The Natural Food Garden.
Rocklin, California:
Prima Publishing, 1992.

Sokolov, Raymond.
Why We Eat What We Eat.
New York: Summit Books, 1991.

Index

ACKNOWLEDGMENTS

Like a garden filled with plants from many sources, a book grows with the nurture, gifts, and knowledge of many friends, advisors, experts, and professionals. ¶ We want to thank A. Cort Sinnes, gardener, illustrator, author, and tomato expert, for his generous friendship and unselfish willingness to share his expertise. Faith, who photographed tomatoes all over America would like to thank Susan and Franz, Dave and Debbie, the Ludlow family, and all the passionate tomato growers who shared their time and opened their gardens. We thank the gardeners who grew the delicious and beautiful tomatoes on these pages: Jill Cole, Stephanie Delmont, Stuart Dickson, Carl Duncan, Susan Duncan, Keith Jones, Renee Post, Petal and Everett Turner, and Estelle and Ron Watts. Also thanks to Wendy Krupnik for advice, and to Nancy Garrison, Cooperative Extension Agent, and Hazel White, horticultural editor, for close reading to weed out errors. Buon gusto to Karen Frerichs, often up to her elbows in tomatoes to test the recipes. ¶ A thank-you to Bill LeBlond, Leslie Jonath, and Laura Lovett, of Chronicle Books, as well as Carey Charlesworth, who, although transplanted to Michigan, kept up the work to prune the manuscript. Our thanks to the designers, Bob Aufuldish and Kathy Warinner, who took a manuscript as unruly as a Sweet 100 tomato vine and fit it to their elegant design. ¶ Finally, we want to thank our friends and family, especially Daniel and Arann, Mimi's sons—who restrained themselves from eating the photo stars—and Bruce, Faith's sweet honey.

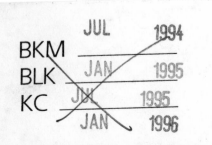